TEACH YOUR CHILD TO RIDE A BIKE IN 10 EASY STEPS!

Shawn Tunis

Contents

INTRODUCTION

Welcome! Teaching a child to ride a bike can be an exercise in exhaustion and frustration for parents as well as a frightening and intimidating experience for children. This book offers a complete, step-by-step, "no tears no fears", and an easy-to-follow system on how to teach a child to ride a bike. By following these easy, progressive, logical steps, your end result will be a child's mastery of bike riding, accompanied by smiling faces in parents and children alike.

My name is Shawn Tunis and I am the mom of fraternal twins, born in 2011. As anyone with twins may know, everything happens in **2's**. So just imagine trying to teach twins to ride a bike ...at the same time! It was so much worse than potty training two kids at a time. Maybe.

The "old school" way of teaching your child to ride a bike (and the way I, and maybe you learned, unfortunately) goes something like this...

Your parent, usually Dad, loads you onto your bike, balances you, pushes you to get you going, runs alongside you, holding you upright until they are gasping for breath, then finally gives you one good shove in the back, and yells **"PEDAL!!"**

Sound familiar? If you too learned this way, you know how this usually ends. A crash... tears... crying... and the inevitable, *"I give up. I NEVER want to learn how to ride a bike!!"* As a parent, it can be excruciating for you and for your child, terrifying. Good luck with the old-school method. The results are exhaustion, frustration, tears, and fear of getting on a bike.

Consider this. Riding a bike requires the mastery of 4 distinct skills: **BALANCE, STEERING, PEDALING, AND BRAKING... THE QUADFECTA OF RIDING A BIKE!** The problem with the old-school method is that it requires a child to learn all 4 skills **simultaneously**. Not easy. Let's see you hop on one foot, rub your stomach with one hand, tap your forehead with the other, and wink your left eye... *all at once. Now see if you can get your 5-year-old to do that.*

Our system teaches each of the four skills **independently**, in a logical sequence, adding one skill at a time after the previous one is mastered. It is possible to learn all 4 skills at once, but it usually ends in repeated failure.

For a few years, my husband and I depended heavily on training wheels, with the fear of finally taking off the training wheels slowly creeping upon us. When our twins turned five, we decided it was time. They received new bikes for their 5th birthday, and we started on the journey. My husband and I spent many hours pulling our hair out over the next year trying to teach them the old-school way.

As a mom, my heart sank into my stomach with the fear of them falling off their bikes, envisioning bloody knees, scraped elbows, and painful tears. It was not working, and everyone was miserable. More sadly, my children always dreaded it and were never having fun. They started to equate trying to learn to ride their bikes with punishment.

Wanting to switch gears, so to speak, we put their training wheels back on and started scouring the internet and the app store for the next few months trying to find a new way. We found very little help and grew tired of taking their training wheels on and off while we tried new methods.

As they approached age 6, we were starting to feel a little embarrassed as parents that our kids still did not know how to ride their bikes on their own. Our family bike rides in the neighborhood consisted of us and our almost 6-year-old twins riding their bikes, still equipped with training wheels. So, one day we took the training wheels off for the last time and threw them away so that we were no longer tempted to put them back on.

My husband, ever the analytic scientist, and I, brainstormed and eventually pieced together different ideas on how to teach them. Some of our ideas were based on what we had learned on the internet and some we created from our own imagination and based on the basic laws of physics. With a bit of creativity, a pinch of persistence, and a dash of patience, we created a 10-step system that in retrospect, made teaching them very easy and painless. After just one week of implementing our new system, our twins were riding on their own, and we had fun throughout the process.

It became obvious to us that we could not be the only parents suffering through this trial by ordeal, so we went back and documented all the steps. We desperately wanted to share our system and our success with other parents who may also be experiencing the same struggles.

Our initial attempt to share our system was to create an app through Apple Development, but the entire process became too complex (and expensive!), so we shelved it. Nonetheless, our own personal struggle of teaching our kids to ride a bike was over, and life moved on.

Fast forward five years, we stumbled upon the manuscript on my husband's computer and decided to resurrect it as a short, illustrated book.

So, here we go, and here it is for you and your children! We hope this system works for you as well as it worked for us. As parents, you play a pivotal role in nurturing this essential skill and the sense of freedom that comes with it. This book is designed to empower you with the knowledge, methods, and insights we gained to help your journey not only be successful, but also an incredibly rewarding and memorable experience for both you and your child(ren).

So grab that bicycle, put on those helmets, and enjoy the journey of teaching your child how to ride a bike with our 10 EASY STEPS method. A journey that will be filled with fun, laughter, and a sense of accomplishment that will last a lifetime.

Make it easy! Learning to ride a bike should be fun for the whole family.

Let's go!

REQUIREMENTS FOR THE SYSTEM

There are certain things you cannot cut corners on if you want to succeed. The following are mandatory prerequisites for you and your child before beginning:

- **An age and size-appropriate bike in perfect working order.** Hand-me-down bikes or bikes that a child has grown out of (and they grow out of bike sizes fast) are not the way to go. If you are unsure of the wheel or bike size for your child's age/weight/height, there are many guides available online or in-store by bike manufacturers. We also recommend going simple with the bike. Let's hold off on the 10-speeds and all the fancy mountain bikes for now. You can always buy those later.

- **An age and size-appropriate fully approved bicycle helmet, to be worn at all times**. It always amazes us to see kids riding bikes without helmets! And now with the electric bikes capable of up to 30 mph, it is even more astounding. A discussion of the morbidity of pediatric closed head injury is beyond the scope of this discussion. Let's not go there. You **MUST** make sure your child has an approved and well-fitting bicycle helmet and that they use it

EVERY single time they get on a bike. It only takes one fall. Safety first!

- **A smooth, paved, and traffic-free practice area of sufficient size.** We know you are tempted to go in your own driveway or on the street in front of your house… we suggest not. Your driveway is not likely to be flat or long enough. The street, even if quiet, has many potential hazards. Find the right parking lot and go there when everything is closed, and it is empty, or try a school parking lot on a weekend. Being away from your house has the advantage of having fewer distractions arise. It also gives more purpose to the training… "Hey, let's go down to the parking lot and practice the next Step with our bikes!"

DISCLAIMER

PLEASE READ THIS CAREFULLY. IF YOU USE THIS SYSTEM, IT IS MUTUALLY UNDERSTOOD THAT YOU AGREE TO THE FOLLOWING:

By reading this book and employing this system, the readers of this teaching system agree in advance to use the methods described herein completely at their own risk and to hold the authors, principals, owners, agents, and or assigns of *"Teach Your Child to Ride a Bike In 10 Easy Steps"* completely harmless whatsoever from any and all liability, injuries, or losses suffered to person(s) or property related to the use of this teaching system, or any part or variation thereof, now or at any time in the future. Furthermore, no guarantee is expressed, written, or implied as to the effectiveness of the teaching method described herein.

STEP ONE: REMOVE THE BICYCLE PEDALS

The first of the 4 independent skills (**Balance, Steering, Braking, and Pedaling**) that you want to teach is **BALANCE**.

The best way to teach **Balance** is to allow your child to learn to balance **a little bit at a time and in short intervals**... not all at once like old school. Our sense of balance on two feet is innate, no one really must teach us to walk... one day, we just do it. Balance on two wheels, however, is an acquired skill. There is no evolutionary value to balancing on two wheels. Once your child's brain sees and feels balance on two wheels, however, a little light bulb goes on in their head, and they will have it forever. Hence the old saying, "Just like riding a bike..."

Since we (and your child) already know how to balance on two feet... let's transfer that skill to wheels by using their two feet to learn balance on two wheels.

We are going to let them sit on the bike, put their feet on the ground, have them lift their feet slightly up off the ground, and then let them put their feet right back on the ground as soon as they feel they are losing their balance. It may be only a second or two to start.

If they are going to use their feet to learn balance, you need to take the pedals off the bike... completely. They need to be out of the way for several reasons. There's no pedaling yet anyway, that comes later.

Without the pedals, your child can use their feet on the ground to stay upright at the very earliest instant they lose balance. They already know how to do that with their feet, right? The pedals can't get in the way. **If they are resting their feet on both pedals, the pedals will be too far away from the ground for them to reach with their feet before they lose balance and fall**. No pedals, no complete loss of balance, no falling.

In the beginning, even if they hold their balance on the bike initially for only a second or two... they will get the idea... and they will hold balance with their feet lifted slightly off the ground for longer and longer intervals. They will feel safe learning balance if they can use their feet!

So, let's first remove the pedals from the bike. **However, be careful, the LEFT pedal is reverse threaded!**

The **RIGHT** pedal (while sitting on the bike) will loosen in the expected direction by turning the nut at the base of the pedal **COUNTERCLOCKWISE** while facing the pedal.

*Facing the RIGHT, pedal turn the
nut counterclockwise to loosen.*

The **LEFT** pedal (while sitting on the bike) will loosen in the opposite of the expected direction by turning the nut at the base of the pedal **CLOCKWISE** while facing the pedal.

*Facing the LEFT pedal, turn the
nut clockwise to loosen.*

*If you turn the left pedal nut
counterclockwise you will be
tightening it!*

STEP TWO: LOWER THE SEAT

For your child to learn balance on their bike using their feet with the pedals removed, you must adjust the seat to the correct height. This is most probably going to take a few trial-and-error adjustments as you have your child get on and off the bike until you find the correct height of the seat as described below.

You do not want the seat to be too high. It is too high if only one foot can reach the ground at a time. You want both feet to be able to touch simultaneously. You also do not want the seat so high such that with maximum possible reach only the very tippy toes of each foot touch simultaneously...that's too hard to balance.

On the other hand, you do not want the seat to be too low. You do not want it so low that their knees are bent at 90 degrees, and they can easily place both feet completely flat on the ground. If the seat is too low, they will never transfer their weight from their feet to the seat.

The correct height will allow both feet to comfortably touch the ground and their behind to rest comfortably on the seat. This specific height will allow the child to transition their weight back and forth easily and rapidly from their feet to the seat as they lose and regain their balance. Think about having the seat height adjusted so that there is a 50/50 distribution of their weight between the seat and the ground.

As a rule of thumb, lower the seat so that both of your child's feet can rest lightly **flat on the ground** while seated and their knees are bent at 20-30 degrees.

Seat Too High

Seat Too Low

Correct Seat Height

STEP THREE: BIKE WALKING AND SITTING

In this step, we are starting the **Balance** training in earnest and will, of necessity, add some of the second skill, **Steering**.

With the seat correctly adjusted and the pedals removed, place your child on the bike and allow them to balance and support themselves without your assistance.

You will need a **completely flat** paved surface for this step. Your driveway is likely not long enough, flat enough, and probably has several obstacles or hazards nearby.

Garden beds, hoses, potholes, gravel, and sand will lead to old-school results. Find a parking lot that fits the bill, even if you must drive there.

Next, have your child **practice "walking" the bike** while seated and encourage them to gradually increase the transfer of their weight to the seat.

The call to action here is *"Sit, then walk."* Keep encouraging them to *"sit"* while walking. They might tend to revert to standing and straddling the seat as they move forward such that they are simply walking with the bike between their legs, so *"Sit"* is your **keyword**. Keep encouraging them to put their behind and weight down on the seat and use their feet only to stay upright and move slowly forward.

Correct Seat Height for Bike Walking

If they continue to walk the bike while straddling the seat and all of their weight is on their feet, then they are not learning balance and the seat may be too low. The walking motion here should be only to propel the bike forward rather than effect a transfer of weight from foot to foot as in normal walking. This walking motion should progress to **"tippy-toe"** walking with most of their weight on the seat.

Bike Walking is accomplished when your child gets on their bike, sits down, instinctively puts their weight on the seat without prompting, and propels forward with a non-weight bearing walking motion.

Once your child can **Bike Walk** while fully seated, with all body weight on the seat, and can travel a significant distance on a flat surface, proceed to the next step.

As you probably realize, this step incorporates the philosophy behind "balance bikes". We like the idea. We like the idea so much, we use it. But with our system, you can use a real bike as a balance bike for the short time necessary to learn balance. Or you can spend the money on a separate balance bike, use it for a short time, and then you will have to buy a real bike anyway.

STEP FOUR: USE THE BRAKES

Teach Your Child How to Stop!

How many times does the old-school method end up in an encounter with a mailbox or a hedge? Teaching a child how to use the brakes was kind of an afterthought with the old-school method... all we were really concerned about was getting up and getting going.

Stopping was the last thing we were thinking about. *"Oh, don't worry… they'll stop…. eventually"* is not a good strategy, to say the least. So next, **<u>let's teach your child how to stop</u>**.

Your child's bike may have hand controls for front and rear brakes, or it may have rear coaster brakes engaged by pedaling in reverse. Either will work fine in the long run, but hand lever control brakes are preferable if you are just buying the bike.

If your child's bike has hand control levers, then instruct and practice using the brakes in this section.

Since we do not have any pedals on the bike, your child can't pedal in reverse to use coaster brakes, so if your child has coaster brakes, we will add the braking skill later during **STEP SEVEN: "Both Feet Up!".**

Now is the time to learn how to use the brakes, with their feet on the ground, no pedaling, so they can learn how to stop **BEFORE** they get up to speed. You can't start teaching your child how to stop **AFTER** they are going like a bat out of hell. Seems pretty obvious, but again, another failure of the old-school method.

Learning and practicing stopping with the brakes during **Bike Walking** should continue to be on a flat surface. We don't want any speed yet, only as much speed as your child can create Bike Walking.

Remember one of the most challenging times to maintain balance is the instant when coming to a complete stop. **<u>Bike Walking, stop with brakes, maintain balance</u>**…

practice with your child until there is no wobble after the stop.

Once you see your child instinctively reach for the brakes without prompting, you are ready for the next step.

STEP FIVE: BIKE GLIDING

This Step is a natural progression and extension of Bike Walking. You should remain on a flat surface.

Now that your child is bike walking, with most of their weight on the seat, using their feet for balance and to propel slowly forward, and knows how to stop we advance to **Bike Gliding**.

In **Bike Gliding** your child will learn to maintain longer intervals of sustained balance and will also pick up a little speed. In **STEP FIVE**, your child will also gain skill in steering without specific attention to that skill. Steering is perhaps the most intuitive of the 4 skills to be learned and many children have learned it already from tricycles or other toddler vehicles.

While fully seated and walking, encourage your child to take big, long exaggerated steps as if Gliding. **Between steps, both feet should be off the ground for short intervals**. One way to encourage Gliding is to ask your child to reach out ahead with their leading foot before putting it down and stretch it out behind as far they can through the step.

Bike Gliding

Bike Gliding

Your child will pick up a little more speed when Gliding, even on a flat surface. I think you can see how this is coming together gradually piece by piece. We now have intervals of Balance, small Steering corrections, and Braking at slow speeds... all at once.

Bike Gliding is the Step that you will perhaps spend the most time with. **<u>This step needs to be mastered</u>**. When your child becomes frustrated that he or she cannot get going fast enough by Gliding, and they can take long Glide steps with both feet off the ground for long distances, you are ready for the next Step.

STEP SIX: RAISE THE SEAT

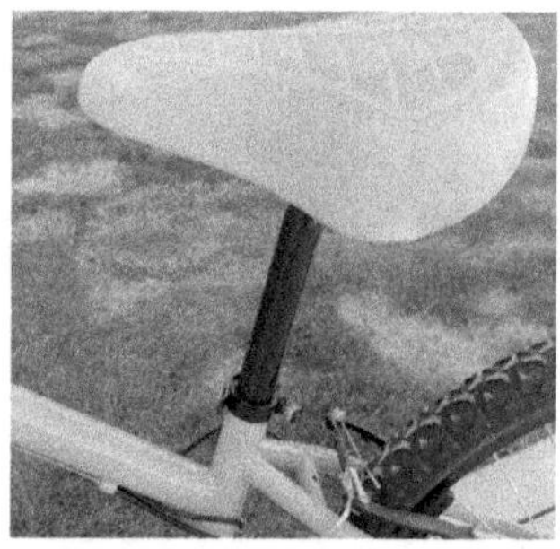

Now that your child can **Balance** nearly all the time while moving slowly forward, it is time to rely on their newly discovered sense of balance on two wheels!

You should **RAISE THE SEAT** back up to a point where only your child's tippy toes can touch the ground while seated. If your child wants to stand, they will have to get off the seat and straddle the bike. Only by leaning the bike to one side slightly should they be able to get all of one foot on the ground while seated.

This change in height still allows them to get enough traction on the ground with their toes to propel forward as in Gliding, but both feet are nearly off the ground. Just as when you lowered the seat, you may have to make several adjustments with your child getting on and off the bike before setting the final correct height.

STEP SEVEN: BOTH FEET UP

Resume **Bike Gliding** at the new seat height on a flat surface AND encourage longer and longer glides and increasing speed.

Once Gliding is easy, long, and brisk you want your child to
get, *"BOTH FEET UP!"* – That's your **Call for Action**!

"BOTH FEET UP!"

Have your child practice repeated passes of the long Glide
with **BOTH FEET UP** and see how long they can maintain
balance.

As the **BOTH FEET UP** Glides get longer you should occasionally call out ***"USE THE BRAKES AND STOP"***.

If your child's bike has coaster brakes which are engaged by reverse pedaling (there are no pedals on the bike yet!) you will not be able to introduce braking until **STEP NINE** and a repeat of **STEP EIGHT** with the pedals installed. No worries.

Your child will most likely not develop enough speed on a flat surface at this point anyway and should easily glide to a stop. Be especially prudent, however, about having a large enough practice area without obstacles to practice BOTH FEET UP if your child has coaster brakes and has not learned the braking skill yet.

With long Glides, they will have just enough speed to make the experience of braking meaningful, even if not necessary, so you should intertwine hand braking practice while long gliding with BOTH FEET UP.

We had friendly contests between our twins to see who could do the longest BOTH FEET UP Glide! (Give siblings any chance to compete against each other and you won't get any arguments, especially when it comes to twins!) Laughing and having fun while learning to ride a bike was a pleasant change from our failed old-school attempts.

Once a distance is achieved during which your child maintains balance for 30 feet or more, makes mild corrections in steering, and can apply the brakes on demand, then they are ready for the next Step.

STEP EIGHT: DOWNHILL GLIDING

For this Step, **Downhill Gliding,** you will need to find a 50-100 foot evenly paved surface free of obstacles with a **<u>slight downhill decline</u>**. It may be a portion of your original practice area, or you may have to find a new one. It can be a neighborhood street if selected carefully and is monitored by a parent at each end.

How much downhill decline? Not much, perhaps 5-10 degrees. The idea is **NOT** to get your child going downhill fast, rather, it is to allow gravity to propel them downhill when they lift their feet rather than them having to use their tippy toes to maintain forward motion as before.

Think of it this another way. If you were sitting on your bike at the top of the grade and you lifted your feet off the ground, would you immediately start rolling down the hill? If yes, it's too steep. You want to the slope such that your child must tippy-toe slightly to initiate forward momentum, but then has enough forward motion to go all the way down the slope without supplying additional toe power.

If they have coaster brakes and did not learn or practice braking in **STEP FOUR**, make sure you do **not** select too steep a slope! The correct slope for downhill gliding should not require brakes to stop, they should run out of gas on their own. We will add coaster brakes in **STEP NINE** and a repeat of **STEP EIGHT**.

Our Downhill Gliding Venue was a back street with 3 cars per day traffic and one parent always posted at both the start and finish lines.

When in doubt, start with the slightest decline and graduate to a steeper incline if you need to.

Once your child can Glide down the entire slope maintaining balance with **BOTH FEET UP,** while making minor steering corrections to stay straight, and using handbrakes on command to slow down or stop at the end of the slope, they are ready for the next Step.

Don't rush to the next Step or go to the next Step after one session, even if your child has mastered this. Spend some time practicing **Downhill Gliding** in at least 3 separate sessions. Repetition creates muscle memory and better coordination of separate skills.

Every Step is important, but <u>**Downhill Gliding is a Biggie**</u>! Plus, they'll have fun too!

STEP NINE: REINSTALL THE PEDALS

The reverse of **STEP ONE**.

Remember! After you thread the pedal into the pedal arm:

- Facing the **RIGHT** pedal, turn the lock nut **CLOCK-WISE** to tighten

- Facing the **LEFT** pedal, turn the lock nut **COUNTER-CLOCKWISE** to tighten

- If you get confused, refer to the pictures in **STEP ONE**, and do the reverse.

STEP TEN: SUPPORT, START, LAUNCH – PEDAL

THE GRAND FINALE.

Congratulations, you made it this far! Hopefully without any old-school challenges! I think we have already learned that there are better ways to get your cardio than running beside a bike gasping for breath and yelling commands at a terrified child.

NOTE: *For children with coaster brakes, go back and repeat* **STEP EIGHT** *with pedals installed.*

Instead of **BOTH FEET UP** during **DOWNHILL GLIDING**, they will now put their feet on the pedals.

Stand next to the bike with your child before their first downhill glide with pedals installed and manually demonstrate how the coaster brake works by pushing down on the right backward-facing pedal.

Right pedal facing backward

- Start the Downhill gliding passes with the **RIGHT** pedal facing backward in the same position it was when you showed them how the brake works

- Practice Downhill gliding while braking during or at the end of the slope by asking your child to push down on backpedal

- Once they can use the pedals to brake during downhill gliding, come back to **STEP TEN** here

Go back to your flat practice area, we don't need gravity anymore, we are going to add locomotion!

The following steps are intuitive to you and me, but they are broken down in detail so that you can explain each step to your child so they perform each one as an independent act.

We suggest that you go through each step carefully with them so that they will do it the same way each time.

a)   Have your child straddle their bike while standing with both feet on the ground.

b)   Have them walk the bike forward until the **RIGHT** pedal is facing forward.

c)   Have them lean the bike slightly to the **LEFT**, sit on the bike, and maintain balance with their **LEFT** foot flat on the ground.

d)   Pick the **RIGHT** foot up and place it on the **RIGHT** pedal while maintaining their balance with the **LEFT** foot still on the ground.

e)   Balance your child upright on the bike using both your hands on the back of the seat from behind while straddling the rear wheel so that your child is fully seated, upright, with both feet on pedals at a standstill with the front wheel pointed straight. You can hold the back wheel between your knees or legs if you need additional leverage to keep the bike upright with your child fully seated.

f)   **You are ready to _LAUNCH_!** With gentle pressure from behind (**NOT A SHOVE!**) begin walking, holding the seat (or the child's waist on both sides) and pushing your child forward on the bike while increasing walking pace.

g)   Ask them to start pedaling by pushing their **RIGHT** foot down on the pedal. **KEEP** walking and holding the seat or their waist until you have reached a brisk pace or a speed that would be about the same as their Downhill Gliding.

NO RUNNING! YOU DON'T NEED TO!

h) Then release and **LAUNCH**! Your **<u>Only Keyword</u>** now is *"Pedal!"* They already have the other 3 skills!

YOU DID IT!

BALANCE, STEERING, PEDALING, AND BRAKING… THE QUADFECTA OF RIDING A BIKE!

NOTE: If your child is more comfortable with their **LEFT** foot on the pedal to start off, simply switch **RIGHT** and **LEFT** in the steps above.

LASTLY: The exhilaration the child experiences on their first real bike ride, however short, may temporarily over-shadow their memory of how to use the brakes… LOL!

We suggest posting a parent at the finish line for possible assistance with stopping or maintaining balance when coming to a full stop.

Sometimes children must be reminded to ***"Put Your Foot on the Ground"*** at the finish line as well.

Double the Joy with Twins in 2017! One week after using our method to teach them how to ride their bikes.

CONCLUSION

There's an undeniable thrill in watching your child(ren) pedal their way to independence. Those first wobbly moments, the triumphant cries of ***"Look, Mom, I'm doing it!"*** and the eventual joy of exploring the world on two wheels are memorable milestones in any parent and child's journey.

Teaching your child to ride a bike is more than just a rite of passage or just balancing on two wheels. You not only impart a valuable life lesson, it's a gift that fosters a love for adventure, health, and exploration that can last a lifetime. It's about fostering confidence, independence, and a deep connection between you and your child(ren).

As they pedal their way into the world on their own two wheels, they will carry with them the lessons learned and the cherished moments shared as a family.

Now go explore the world together and create some lasting memories on family bike rides.

Thank you for reading! *If you enjoyed this book, please leave a review on the forum of purchase.*

-Shawn Tunis, Author

www.ingramcontent.com/pod-product-compliance
Lightning Source LLC
Chambersburg PA
CBHW071458150726
48000CB00006B/2615